THIS BOOK IS A GIFT FROM

_____

TO

_____

ON THE OCCASION

_____

DATE

_____

SIGN

_____

THE CHILD THAT GOD USES

COPYRIGHT © MAY 2019 BY:

Femi Emmanuel Bamidele & Janie Sue

RECORD BEARER MOVEMENT
17, Taiwo Olaleye Street, Agodo, Egbe
Lagos, Nigeria.

Tel: +234-805 2204 664, +234 -806 9837 449
E-mail: recordbearerglobal@gmail.com,
femibamidele2020@gmail.com
Twitter: @FEMIBAMIDELE202
Facebook: FEMI EMMANUEL BAMIDELE

USA CONTACT:
Apostle Ruben Su'e/Prophetess Janie Su'e

LIGHT OF THE WORLD MINISTRIES
SAN ANTONIO TEXAS
USA
Email: Janiemln@yahoo.com

CONTENTS

INTRODUCTION page 01

1
SAMUEL: THE PROPHET   page 04

2
JOSIAH: THE KING AND REFORMER   page 12

3
NAAMAN'S MAID: A DESTINY HELPER   page 19

4
DAVID : THE SHEPHERD'S BOY   page 26

NEW WORDS   page 32

INTRODUCTION

We have come to understand lately that God has a plan for every child in His end time agenda for the church in the nations of the earth. Children are of great priority to God in this last move of the Holy Spirit across the Nations. God has an eternal heart of love, compassion and value for children. He has used them before, and still want to use them again. Act 2:17 clearly spelt it out that our sons and daughters shall prophesy, and young men shall see visions. Children are not left out in God's last day work. The bible is God's story book of redemption. And our God is the same yesterday, today and forever and what He did then, He can do again. God using children in the bible shows that children are no spectators in the drama of salvation history, but important vessels in fulfilling the mandate of God on earth in this last hour. Let us open our hearts and learn from the story of these four children that God used in the bible. Samuel, Josiah, Naaman's maid and David. May you be the next child God will use for His glory in your generation as you encounter Him reading through the pages of this book in Jesus name.

It is our earnest plead, parents (awaiting inclusive) to pray all the prayers point raised in each of the chapter for the children.

Happy Reading!

Femi & Janie

1
SAMUEL:
THE PROPHET

The Story Of His Birth

Once upon a time in Shiloh, there was a woman in the days of the Prophet Eli called Hannah who was barren but became tired of her barrenness and entered a covenant deal with the Lord. She asked the Lord for Samuel and promised God that, if God could give her "this man child", she would give him back to the Lord. Every child is a

Hannah cried to Eli

"Where it came to pass, when the time was come about after Hannah had conceived, that she bare a son, and called his name Samuel, saying, because I have asked him of the Lord."
1 Samuel 1:20.

man child" but not all reveal the purpose of the "man child".

Samuel was a child that was asked of the Lord. Hannah fulfilled her promise, she came back to

Shiloh and lent Samuel to the Lord all the days of his life.

> "Therefore also I have lent him to the Lord; as he live he shall be lent to the Lord. And he worshipped the Lord there." 1 Samuel 1:28.

Samuel was born

Hannah is an example of a praying and goodly mother. From the time she first desired to have a child, she prayerfully and purposefully presented her child before the Lord. She regarded her son as a precious gift from God and expressed her intentions to fulfill her vow by dedicating him to the Lord for the rest of his life.

Samuel heard the voice of God

Samuel grew up in the presence of the Lord, heard God's voice as a child and revealed God's mind to Eli the High priest.

It was believed that Samuel was between the age of seven and twelve; he was a young servant to Eli the

High Priest. He was confused as he hears the voice calling to him. Eli his master called him to respond to the voice of God with a willingness to listen. Samuel received a message that revealed the heart of the nation and particularly, the household of Eli.

Samuel was used as a prophet and judge in the land of Israel for forty years, the testimony of his ministry as a prophet was that, none of his word went without coming to pass.

The key thing we want to focus on in this story is that, Samuel was looked for and called by God at a very tender age. He answered that call and also fulfilled the purpose of God for his life. He came when the Lord was in need of a vessel to use to replace the rebellious house of Eli and his two sons.

LESSON TO LEARN FROM THE STORY

- You also can be another prophet Samuel that God will use to spark a revival in your generation.
- God is still interested in you to use as a child's prophet, evangelist, teacher and pastor.
- God is still in the business of calling and using children to execute His judgment against wickedness in the land.
- Despite the waywardness of the two sons of Eli, Samuel stood his ground for the Lord, even in his childhood ministry.
- Samuel refused to be corrupted in the midst of heavy corruption of the ministers of his days.
- He was accessible to God's voice, visions and divine revelations.
- Samuel lived a godly life in such a time in history when living godly as a minister was difficult in the life of the sons of his mentor- Hophni and Phinehas.

LET US PRAY

Father use me as a child for your glory in Jesus name.

Father make me another prophet Samuel of my generation in Jesus name.

Father let your word be revealed to me in Jesus name.

Give me a clear understanding of your voice as a child in Jesus name.

2
JOSIAH:
THE KING AND REFORMER

BACKGROUND OF JOSIAH

Josiah was the last of the righteous kings of Judah. He became a king at a tender age of eight and reigned for thirty one years. At an early age he began earnestly to seek the Lord and four years later he began to purge Judah of false worship. Jedidah, the daughter of Adaiah of Boscath, begot him and his father was called Amon. The testimony of his father was that he did evil in the sight of the Lord.

HIS TESTIMONY AS A CHILD

2kings 22:2 says this about him;
"And he did that which was right in the sight of the Lord, and walked in all the way of David his father, and turned not aside to the right hand or to the left.

As the temple was being repaired Hilkiah the high priest in his days found the book of the law written by Moses. His discovery of God's word ensured a given measure of spiritual reformation were accomplished throughout the land. The prophets Jeremiah and Habakkuk aided Josiah in his attempt to bring the people back to God in his spiritual reforms mission.

Josiah was raised for reverence for God, and acted swiftly against pagan idolatry. Even though he became a king at the age of eight, but was nurtured in the wisdom of God. At the age of sixteen he began to clear the pagan worship places from the land.

Josiah was mightily used of the Lord as a child reformer who was also the youngest king in the history of Israel.

His dedication to God reveals that a young child (person) can have a zeal for the Lord and His cause or greater than that of many older adults.

In such a time like this where of high level of modernized idolatry is seen as norm, the Lord is in need of a child just as He sought for a man. The Lord is also seeking for that child that will be available for His use to destroy the works of the enemies in this last hour.

LESSONS TO LEARN FROM JOSIAH'S STORY

*Even though his father did evil in the sight of the Lord, yet he chose to do the right thing in God's sight instead. He did not walk or follow the evil ways of his father Amon.

*It taught us that, living and being surrounded by evil people and practices is not an excuse to do evil. You can still choose to be different.

*Josiah chose to walk in the right way of the Lord even when the only option and example for him to follow as a child are the evil ways of his father. He did not repeat the fatal errors of his evil father.

*As a child he stood for righteousness and, that which was God's interest.

*He humbles himself as a child even when he was a king.

*He lived a life that is pleasing to God.

*He was used by God to enforce a spiritual reformation in his life time as a child in the land of Israel.

*He restored the commitment of the nation to the word of God.

*He did not only pull down the altars of Baal but also burnt them.

*Josiah's reforms fulfill the scriptural principle that repentance for specific sins is essential to true revival.

*Whenever genuine repentance comes specific sins will be identified, false believers will be exposed, worldly practices forsaken, and godly standard restored.

LET US PRAY

Father make me another Josiah, the reformer of my generation in Jesus name.

Father use me as an instrument of destroying the works of darkness in my time in Jesus name.

Father use me to restore the worship of the true God wherever I find myself in Jesus name.

Father use me as a child to restore godly standard in any position you will put me as a child.

Father give me grace to seek you with all my heart, to walk in the right way and do the right things in your sight in Jesus name.

NAAMAN'S MAID,
A DESTINY HELPER

3
NAAMAN'S MAID:
A DESTINY HELPER

"Now ,Namaan, captain of the host of the king of Syria, was a great man with his master, and honorable ,because by him the Lord had given deliverance unto Syria: he was also a mighty man in a valour, but he was a leper. And the Syrians had gone out by companies, and had brought away captives out of the land of Israel a little maid; and she waited on Naaman's wife. And she said unto her mistress, would God my lord were with the prophet that is in Samaria! for he would recover him of his leprosy. And one went in, and told his lord, saying, Thus and thus said the maid, that is of the land of Israel." 2 Kings 5:1-4. (KJV)

The record bearer of the story of this maid in the house of Naaman did not even mention her name. She was a nameless one that was used to change the story of Naaman's life. No one would have heard of Naaman's leprosy and his healing if not for her godly and humbly advice to Naaman, the captain of the host of Syria. The bible described her as a little maid of Naaman's wife.

The first thing we noticed from the story was that , she was a little girl. She was also an Israelite but a slave or captive serving as a maid in the house of Naaman. The little maid must have had a godly background and godly heart. Despite the fact, she was taken captive against her wish. She was still concerned about the healing of her boss. She showed concerned at the wit's end over the leprosy of captain Naaman. The military leader or commander in person of Naaman embraced the advice of this young maid to see the prophet Elisha.

His healing would not have been possible if not that he took heed to that little girl advice. The little maid was the destiny helper that Naaman needed to connect to his destiny of total healing from the age-long disease of leprosy. She was the divine instrument that made his healing to be possible.

This is to let us know that a counsel or simple advice can alter a man's destiny. That was what she offered to her master. And because Naaman was also not despising her counsel, he received his total healing. We must never underestimate the power of a good counselor advice.

I remember also that the destiny of king David would have been aborted by the single counsel of Ahitophel if not that king David prayed to God to turn his counsel to foolishness in the hearing of Absalom.

Most wise leaders either in the kingdom or secular world often surround themselves with good advisers or wise counselors. Counsel itself is a spirit from the Lord. One of the gifts that is often been used to powered good and productive advice and counsel is divine wisdom.

May the Lord decorate your life with His wisdom in Jesus name.

LESSONS TO LEARN FROM THE STORY OF NAAMAN'S MAID

- Regardless of our status or position in this life we must not fail to contribute our quota of impact to our generation.
- Irrespective of your challenge, you have been given a gift, something to bless your generation with.
- The little maid was compassionate about her master leprosy. Therefore, it will take a compassionate to be impactful in life.

LET US PRAY

Father make me to make impact in my life time regardless of where I find myself.

Father grant me grace to live by adding value to people lives.

Father endow me with gifts that I need to impact my generation for God in Jesus name

Father help me never to miss any opportunity of doing good to everyone you bring across my way in life in Jesus name.

Father give me a compassionate heart in Jesus name.

DAVID:
THE SHEPHERD'S BOY

Once upon a time, there was a boy in the land of Israel, who never thought to be qualified even by his brethren and father to be anointed as a king. His name is called David. The same was chosen by God to become the king of Israel after God's rejection of Saul as a king.

HIS ORDINATION

The Lord specifically sent Prophet Samuel to go and anoint for him a king whom he has provided among the sons of Jesse. After the

sanctification of the seven sons of Jesse, prophet Samuel could not see any one of them approved by the Lord to be king.

This made him to ask the father to sent for his last son from the bush while all of them would remain standing until he comes. David was anointed in the midst of his brethren by Samuel and the Spirit of the Lord came upon him from that day henceforth. David became the provided king of Israel although not yet enthroned. And after many generations, David is still known as a man after God's heart.

IN WHAT WAY DID GOD USED DAVID AS A BOY

David challenged Goliath, the man who the whole army of Israel feared and could not confront. While the nation trembled in fear of the philistines giant, David refused the armour of King Saul and delivered Israelites from oppression. The teenage boy went on to become a key figure in salvation history.

Therefore, the Goliath that the king and all the army of Israel could not handle, the Lord used the little David to defeat effortlessly. He challenged, conquered and cut off the head of Goliath, the champion of the philistines.

David battle goliath

David anointed by God takes away the reproach of the enemy from the children of Israel. Though, his brothers despised him, and also tried stopping him from fulfilling his destiny yet God used that singular act of killing Goliath to announce him in Israel. King Saul also tried to let him see reasons for him to see his confrontation of Goliath being a boy as an impossible mission. But the young David knew his God and by virtue of his testimony of killing a bear and a lion repeatedly, assured Saul of wasting Goliath as one of those beasts.

David was a shepherd boy with a lion heart, bold and courageous,

David words of faith to Goliath

45 Then said David to the Philistine, Thou comest to me with a sword, and with a spear, and with a shield: but I come to thee in the name of the Lord of hosts, the God of the armies of Israel, whom thou hast defied.

46 This day will the Lord deliver thee into mine hand; and I will smite thee, and take thine head from thee; and I will give the carcases of the host of the Philistines this day unto the fowls of the air, and to the wild beasts of the earth; that all the earth may know that there is a God in Israel.

47 And all this assembly shall know that the Lord saveth not with sword and spear: for the battle is the Lord's, and he will give you into our hands.

48 And it came to pass, when the Philistine arose, and came, and drew nigh to meet David, that David hastened, and ran toward the army to meet the Philistine.

49 And David put his hand in his bag, and took thence a stone, and slang it, and smote the Philistine in his forehead, that the stone sunk into his forehead; and he fell upon his face to the earth.

50 So David prevailed over the Philistine with a sling and with a stone, and smote the Philistine, and slew him; but there was no sword in the hand of David.

I Samuel 17:45-50

LESSONS TO LEARN FROM DAVID'S STORY

*God's uses people regardless of their age to fulfill his purpose.

*Doing exploits in life is not about age but by His anointing (Grace).

*It will take the child whom the Lord has secretly anointed, prepared and provided to handle every Goliath whom the rejected ones before God of any generation cannot confront.

*The solution of a generational problem in or of a nation and be placed by God in the hand of a child that has been anointed for that purpose.

*Just as God sought for a man to stand in the gap, so also, He is seeking for a child to put an end to the arrogance of every Goliath ridiculing His name in the midst of His children.

*You also can be that David, a "man child" after the

heart of God whom the Lord secretly anointed to take away the head of Goliath challenging your family or nation in battle.

*Irrespective of any Goliath (threatening power) that is harassing your families and nations; the anointing to prevail over is in those children with Davidic anointing - giant killing anointing.

*The killing of Goliath by young David was the announcement of David and his family in the land of Israel.

LET US PRAY

*Father make me another David of my generation in Jesus name.

*Father anoint me to bring down every Goliath that is defying your name in my life, family and generation.

*Father anoint my hands to prevail in the battle of life in Jesus name.

*Father use us as generation of children with Davidic anointing in Jesus name.

NEW WORDS

Agenda: A lists of things to do

Priority: A thing that is regarded as more important than others, most important consideration

Mandate: An official order or commission to do something

Dedication: the quality of being committed to a task.

Intention: A thing intended; an aim or plan; goal

Willingness: the state of being prepared to do something; readiness.

Rebellious: showing a desire to resist authority, control, or convention.

Testimony: A testament, proof or evidence

Waywardness: Turned or turning away from what is right or prosper

Wickedness: The quality of being evil or morally wrong

Earnestly: With sincere and intense conviction; seriously or firmly

Purge: Rid something or somebody of an unwanted quality, condition or feeling.

NEW WORDS

Aided: help or support (someone or somebody) in the achievement of something.

Reform: Make changes in something especially in order to improve it.

Modernized: Adapt to modern needs or habits, ideas or methods.

Enforced: Caused by force or necessity; compulsory

Commitment: The quality of being dedicated to a cause

Underestimate: Set too low or underrate

Compassionate: Feeling or showing sympathy and concern for others.

Impactful: Having a major impact or effect

Ordination: It the process by which an individual is consecrated

Sanctification: It is the act or process of acquiring sanctity, of being made or becoming holy

RBM CHILDREN CLASSIC

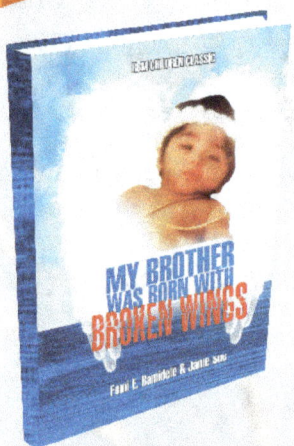

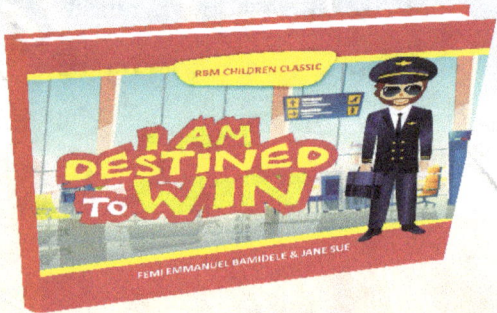

www.ingramcontent.com/pod-product-compliance
Lightning Source LLC
Chambersburg PA
CBHW052129110526
44592CB00013B/1806